Intermediate Piano Solo

Golden Aspens

Joyce Grill

D1503801

Signature Series

Alfred

Golden Aspens

Joyce Grill

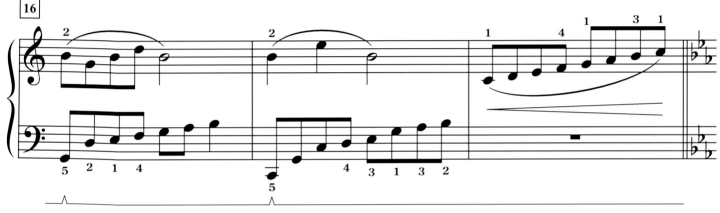

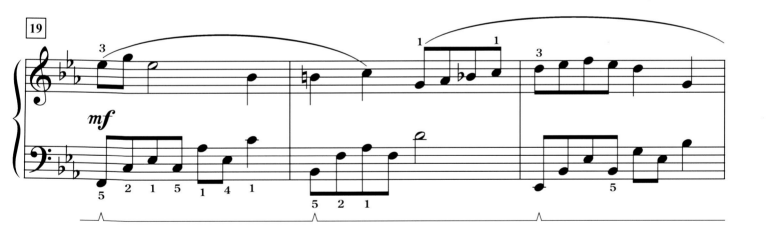

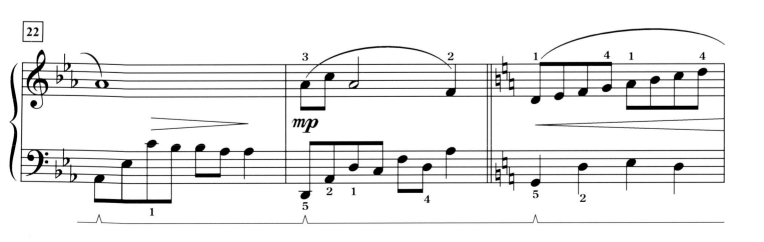

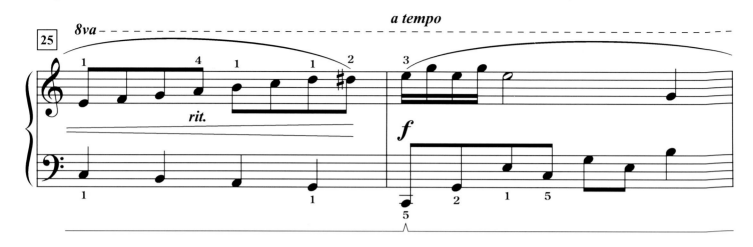

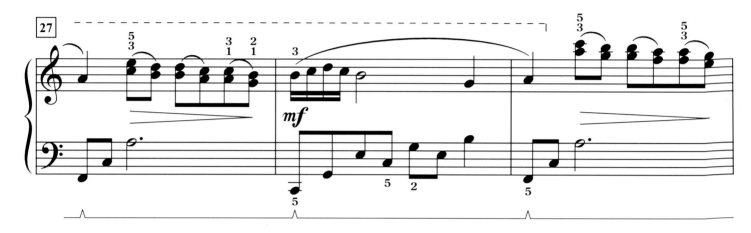

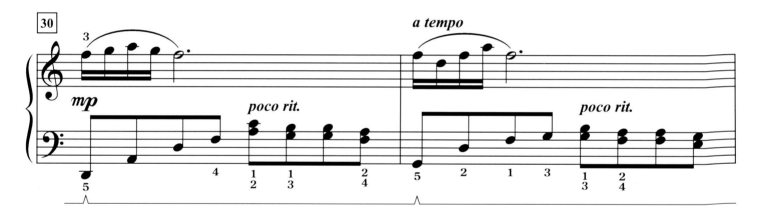

41286 $3.50 in USA

alfred.com

ISBN-10: 0-7390-9730-
ISBN-13: 978-0-7390-97

ISBN 0-7390-9730-X